ASHBURNHAM INSIGHTS

Prophecy

A re-reading of Scripture by
Timothy Pain

KINGSWAY PUBLICATIONS
EASTBOURNE

ISBN 0 86065 486 9

Unless otherwise indicated biblical quotations are from
the Jerusalem Bible, copyright © Darton, Longman & Todd Ltd
and Doubleday & Co. Inc. 1966, 1967, 1968

*Cover photo shows front water
and the main bridge at Ashburnham Place
(colour photograph by Judges Postcards Ltd, Hastings).*

Printed in Great Britain for
KINGSWAY PUBLICATIONS LTD
Lottbridge Drove, Eastbourne, E. Sussex BN23 6NT by
Richard Clay (The Chaucer Press) Ltd, Bungay, Suffolk
Typeset by Nuprint Services Ltd, Harpenden, Herts AL5 4SE

Contents

Foreword to the Series

I am very pleased to commend this series of *Ashburnham Insights* which have come from the pen of Timothy Pain. Those of us who have watched developments at Ashburnham Place over the last few years have been particularly intrigued with the way things have developed. The careful thinking in these volumes comes from a background of faithful believing prayer for many years, and a deep concern for renewal and revival.

When there is an emphasis on experience, and when the subjective element in Christian living is to the fore, there is more need than ever for scriptural foundations. That is why we should be grateful to Tim for the obvious care he has taken to 'test everything', while at the same time to obey the apostolic injunction to 'despise not prophesyings'. Both should play their part in balanced Christian living.

Tim is not afraid to break new ground, and his *Insights* on speaking in tongues will be challenging to those of us who need it. I like the living way he writes, and I am sure these small books will have the wide readership they deserve.

Canon Michael Harper

This series of short books is dedicated to the memory of my father, A. F. Pain (1915-1982).

He emerged from the Deptford slums, without education or refinement, as a natural leader of men. He was radical and traditional, patient and impetuous, obstinate and flexible, gentle and ruthless; loved or loathed by all he met. He faithfully served Christ, the church, his family and the people of Brixton.

Introduction

This series has been inspired by members of the Ashburnham Stable Family. This is a Christian community, part resident at Ashburnham Place (a Christian training centre) and part scattered throughout the villages and small towns of East Sussex. It is our calling to maintain an unbroken 'Chain of Prayer' within the Palladian Stable which is adjacent to Ashburnham Place. We pray, by day and night, for the renewal and spiritual unity of all Christian churches in East Sussex. It is our conviction that the hope of the world lies in the renewal of the church, and as one expression of this we have taken it upon ourselves to share in a serious re-reading of Holy Scripture.

It seems to me that much contemporary teaching is based on experience rather than the Bible. Just as the members of the Stable Family have gained courage to move away from the shallow waters of their varied experiences and traditions, so we urge you to let go and swim with Jesus in the raging torrent of living waters which is eternal life in the Spirit.

The book is humbly offered to the church as my personal re-reading with regard to prophecy. It has been lived in, worked out and written down in community. It is the product of much study and prayer; reading and listening; experimentation and embarrassment; banter and disagreement. Some within the Stable Family still lovingly dissent from a few of my conclusions! Much of the material was originally worked on by the Rev. Edmund Heddle and myself for our conference weekends, when groups take time apart to be with God.

In recent years God has called the Stable Family to new depths of silent listening and bold proclaiming. These I humbly share. They are not the last words on prophecy. Those can never be written. What follows is simply a statement of where God has led this community—thus far. It is our fervent hope and prayer that God will lead us 'farther up and farther in', so that this book becomes an embarrassment to us because of its shallowness and inevitable errors.

These *Ashburnham Insights* have been written with housegroup leaders in mind. One of the great works of the Spirit in the last fifteen years has been the emergence and establishment of house groups. It is my prayer that these four books will aid these leaders in their high and holy calling.

I have tried to write in a way that is simple enough to satisfy the sincere seeker, but sufficiently thorough to persuade those called to teach and lead in the church. The scripture references should all be looked up and examined as you proceed through the text. Bible quotations are normally taken from the Jerusalem Bible.

Any plaudits should be shared between John and Marlis Bickersteth, Helen Brown, Winifred Cox, Edmund Heddle, Gay Hyde, Jo and Susie Marriott, Margery May, Dennis and Pat Nolan, Alan Pain, Barbara Stidwill, Muriel Teideman, Roger and Penny Willcock and my wife Alison. Their prayers, patience, comments, advice, encouragement, work and love have brought the Insights from gestation to publication.

Timothy Pain

The renewal lives by the re-reading of the New Testament.

Cardinal Suenens

Back to the Bible or back to the jungle.

Luis Palau

Our prophesying is imperfect.

St Paul

I like mysteries, but I rather dislike muddles.

E. M. Forster

To will implies delay; therefore, now do.
Hard deeds the body, pain, hard knowledge too,
The mind's endeavours reach; and mysteries
Are like the sun, dazzling, yet plain to all eyes.
Keep the truth which thou hast found. . . .

John Donne

Shall I, for fear of feeble man,
Thy Spirit's course in me restrain?
Or undismay'd in deed and word,
Be a true witness to my Lord?

No, let man rage! Since Thou wilt spread
Thy shadowing wings around my head:
Since in all pain Thy tender love
Will still my sweet refreshment prove.

George Whitefield

Prophecy

Few words arouse in the mind such a wide divergence of ideas as does the word 'prophecy'. To some, prophecy is restricted to teaching about the end times and second coming of Jesus Christ. To others, the immediate impression is of hard-to-find and little-read books at the back end of the Old Testament. To still more, the image is of some bearded, biblical fortune teller-cum-weather forecaster—a sort of primeval Russell Grant! And a fourth group identifies prophecy with 'radical' theology and a political position to the left of centre. Perhaps the most pathetic caricature of prophecy is the well meaning but weedy individual who utters in a quivering voice, 'Oh, my children, I do saith unto thee that I am well pleaseth withst thou. Yes, verily; even verily, verily; my love ist pourethed out upon thee.' Are any of these the true picture of prophecy?

Some people argue that prophecy ceased with the completion of the New Testament, others that it fizzled out as the church was corrupted by institutionalism. Some say that prophecy has been restored to the church only in the last twenty-five years. A few propose a definition of prophecy which suggests that all Christians are prophesying, and have been prophesying, right through the centuries. Where does the truth lie?

I will posit a broad understanding of prophecy: that it is 'to hear or see what God is saying and pass it on'. Yet I will also attempt to establish a particular place for the 'gift of prophecy' within Christian worship. At the time of writing, this gift is only embryonic, yet nevertheless it is essential for the building together and building up of the church. I will attempt to describe two parallel functions of the two types of prophet who ought to be recognized today.

First, there is the 'office' of prophet, which is held by the individual who functions occasionally or regularly, often in isolation, as a divinely called and divinely inspired speaker. He (with my profuse apologies to Huldah, Miriam, Deborah, Noadiah, Anna, Mrs Isaiah, Philip's four daughters, and more) receives intelligible and authoritative revelations or messages and is impelled to deliver them publicly or privately in oral, written or symbolic form to Christian individuals or communities, or to society and nations. Michael Harper, in the Ashe lecture of 1979, proposed Alexander Solzhenitsyn and Malcolm Muggeridge as epitomes of a prophet today. I would add Mary Whitehouse, Mother Teresa and Bishop Tutu to his list as further examples of those called to the divine office of prophet.

And then there is the 'ministry' of prophet. This is held by the divinely inspired individual who regularly, frequently and publicly exercises the spoken gift of prophecy within the service and meetings of a particular local church. After a period of time he, or she, is recognized as exercising this ministry by the leaders of the church, and is set apart by them to the ministry of prophet. He brings an immediately inspired message of improvement, encouragement or consolation from God to that church. This prophet never functions in isolation, but always in conjunction with at least three other prophets in the church

(see 1 Corinthians 14:29). God's message is established
not from the prophecy of one individual, but from the
prophetic group acting corporately under the influence of
the Spirit of God.

TWO OR THREE PROPHETS
SHOULD SPEAK, AND THE
OTHERS SHOULD WEIGH
CAREFULLY WHAT IS SAID.

Prophets and Prophecy in the Old Testament

What was a prophet?

In the Old Testament a prophet was commonly called a 'man of God'. Moses—the supreme prophet of the Old Testament—was the first to merit this title (Deuteronomy 33:1) but he was followed by others, both famous and anonymous: 1 Samuel 2:27, 1 Samuel 9:6, 1 Kings 13, 1 Kings 17:18, 1 Kings 20:28, 2 Kings 4:7, 2 Chronicles 25:7–9, Nehemiah 12:24. This choice of title shows the difference of character which set them apart from ordinary men.

The prophets were also known as servants. The phrase 'servant of God' is only given to Moses, but 'his', 'your' and 'my' are used of the other prophets. 2 Kings 17:13 and Ezra 9:11 show the servant relationship they enjoyed with God. They were God's mouthpieces, under orders to relay his message and not to alter it in any way.

The three Hebrew words—*nabi*, *roeh* and *hozeh*—seem to be used synonymously. *Nabi* has the idea of calling. It can mean either one who is called or one who calls. *Roeh* and *hozeh* are different forms of 'to see'. A prophet sees God, sees what God is doing, sees events and is seen by men. These three words convey the picture of a prophet as a man called by God, calling to men from God, calling to God for men. He is one who sees those things which remain invisible to other men and is himself clearly seen by men. There can be no such creature as a silent, invisible prophet!

How did they become prophets?

They did not choose the career; they had to be chosen by Almighty God. Some were chosen before their birth. All the different accounts of the calling of a prophet demonstrate the power of God's call. The men had to choose either to set aside what they were doing and commence something which appeared both hard and unpleasant, or to disobey Almighty God. In one sense God *had* to call the prophets. No one with any sense would have volunteered! They got in trouble with men if they spoke God's word and in bigger trouble with God if they remained silent. Exodus 3:1–4:17, Isaiah 6, Jeremiah 1:4–19, Ezekiel 3, Hosea 1:2, Amos 7:14–15 and Jonah 1:1 are some of the biblical accounts of the calling of a prophet.

The primary object of the call was not to send them off on a divine errand, but to summon them into the presence of the holy God. When they had stood before him they could stand before men. Whilst there, God would whisper his secrets into their ears. God never did, or does, anything without first revealing his intention to his servants the prophets. Having faced God and received their commission, they were sent to particular men and nations with a unique message. This is seen in 1 Kings 22, Jeremiah 23:22 and Amos 3:7.

What was their message?

Reconciliation

The main thrust of their message was always 'get right with God'. They pronounced warnings about the future which they validated by quoting examples of God's dealings in the past. They consistently called the ungodly to repentance by painting a picture of the wrath to come. They presented the anger of God against individuals and nations, and attempted to introduce the fear of God into each situation. As far as the Old Testament prophets were concerned, reconciliation with God was only possible when people were aware of God's anger and had a right fear towards him. These reconciliation prophecies form the bulk of Old Testament prophecy. Amos 5, Zephaniah 1:14—2:3 and Hosea 5 are typical of this sort of prophecy.

Occasionally the prophets spoke in terms of future blessing and called the godly to holiness. They charged God's people to live according to their calling. This is still the message, 'get right with God', but it is expressed in a different way. Isaiah 2:2–5 is such a passage.

Social justice

Moses was the supreme prophet of the Old Testament. His divinely inspired emphasis on social justice runs through the Mosaic Law, for example, Leviticus 19:9–18 and Deuteronomy 23:15–25. This message was underlined by all the later prophets, but especially by Amos (Amos 2:6–7, 4:1–3, 8:4–8) and in 2 Chronicles 28:9–15 where the prophet Oded gives not only a command not to mistreat the poor, the strangers, the weak, the widows and the orphans, but also a warning not to be apathetic about their plight and an order to make adequate provision for them.

Prediction and proclamation

The prophets constantly reminded the people of what God had done. At times they almost functioned as court historians. They used the past to reveal God's nature and then would state what God was about to do. This was not inspired guesswork, but divine revelation. They did not make projections. They prophesied—that is, they spoke what God had said. In particular, they called people away from false gods to the one true God. They did this by reminding the people how God had dealt in the past with those who had departed from the sole worship of Yahweh. Monotheism was their monotonous theme. This can be seen in Isaiah 41:21–23 and Isaiah 45:20–22.

They would also announce an event which was about to take place in the near future, and, in the same breath, with the same words, they would predict another event which was totally beyond their ken, maybe a thousand years away. Moses, in Deuteronomy 18:15, reassured the people about what would happen when he had died. He had Joshua in mind as the prophet 'from among yourselves'. Yet this was a glorious prediction about another 'Yeshua' from Nazareth some 1500 years later—Jesus, the prophet mighty in word and deed. Isaiah 7:14 is another example of this type of 'now and then' prophecy.

National events

Some prophets played a leading role in national events. The first two kings, Saul and David, were also prophets. From then on there was a close link between the anointed king and the anointed prophet. Sometimes the king would consult the prophet to find out God's thoughts or take divine advice, 1 Kings 14:1–18, 2 Kings 6:21–23, 8:7–8, 2 Chronicles 34:22–28. At other times the prophet was sent to confront the ruler with a message from God, 1 Kings 11:29–39, 13:1–10, 18:1–2.

Intercession

One of the prophetic functions was to intercede with God for situations and people. Abraham, the first prophet, is described as being able to plead successfully with God and change the situation (Genesis 20:7). It is the very nature of a prophet to intercede. He is the one who calls to God and is called into the very presence of Almighty God for consultation. Jethro suggested to Moses that he should make this his priority and Moses implemented his advice (Exodus 18:19; Numbers 27:5). Time and again the prophets became known as such powerful intercessors that kings would beg them to plead with God on their behalf (1 Kings 13:6; 2 Kings 19:4; Zechariah 7:1–3).

How were they inspired?

Their two main means of inspiration were the word of God and the Spirit of God. Some prophets, for example, Moses, were principally 'word inspired' prophets and others, for example, Elijah, were 'Spirit inspired' prophets. As will be seen later, this difference in inspiration continues today. Those with the 'office' of prophet tend to be inspired by the 'word' and those with the 'ministry' of prophet are more usually inspired by the 'Spirit'. This distinction in inspiration should not be overstressed.

The word of the Lord

I cannot read the Old Testament without being amazed at the dynamic impact of the word of the Lord upon the prophets. 'The Lord Yahweh speaks: who can refuse to prophesy?' (Amos 3:8). 'The word of the Lord came to' is the most frequent phrase which describes this mode of inspiration. 'Came to' is better rendered as either 'became actively present to'; or, more simply, 'was to'. It describes an internal awareness of God's message that grows over a period of time: over a month in Zechariah 1:1, although sometimes the inspiration was more immediate, as in Zechariah 1:7. On other occasions this internal prompting stemmed from events as ordinary as the sight of an almond tree, two baskets of figs, or a visit to a local factory or building site (Jeremiah 1:11; Jeremiah 24; Jeremiah 18:1–4; Amos 7:7). It seems that God unveils his word in the intimacy of private fellowship with the prophet, rather than with a sudden flash of illumination. This is inspiration as the result of meditation, reflection, observation and study.

Habakkuk 1:1 describes the *massa* of the Lord. Some translations render this as 'message' or 'oracle', but literally it is a load or burden. It conjures up the picture of the Lord allowing the prophet to feel what he feels. Isaiah often felt the burden of the Lord about other nations, (Isaiah 13–23). In Jeremiah 23:33–40, Jeremiah identified the false prophets as a burden of the Lord. Again, it appears to be a growing awareness with a measured, calculated, controlled delivery, rather than a spontaneous outburst.

The Spirit

Scripture teaches such a real association between the Spirit and prophecy that it cannot be overstated. Numbers 11:29 is the first hint of a link. The experiences of Saul in 1 Samuel 10 and 1 Samuel 19:18–24 show that the descent of the Spirit in the Old Testament led to spontaneous, temporary, unsought and unavoidable prophecy. Micah 3:8 suggests that the Spirit was not only the source of inspiration but also gave the courage with which to deliver the revelation. The prophecy of Joel 2:28 makes it quite clear that the reception of the Spirit should result in the activity of divine prophesying. This is instant inspiration for immediate delivery.

A Prophetic Dream

I first met Alison in September 1971. We went out together until July 1973 when we split up after months of continuous rows. God brought us back together as a couple in April 1975 after separately filling us both with his Holy Spirit. We assumed this would improve our relationship and got engaged in October 1975. But by the following Easter we were back in the old cycle of regular rows and reconciliations, and wondered if we should break off the engagement.

My regular Bible reading brought me, that Easter, to Matthew's nativity account. For the first time I noticed how God used five different dreams as guidance. This was a new thought. As I chewed it over I became convinced that God would speak to me that very night through a dream. I assumed it would deal with my career. So that night I lay awake waiting. And nothing happened.

The following morning I felt embarrassed at my stupidity and visited Alison to mention my foolish thoughts. Ten minutes after entering her home, the telephone rang. It was a friend whom we had not seen for two years—a lapsed Christian—to tell Alison about her strange dream of the night before, which had featured Alison and myself!

The gist was that we were walking up a slippery mountain, always striding three steps forward then sliding two steps back, but that, eventually, we made it to the top. Our friend thought it screamingly funny. We were awestruck and took heart to press on to marriage.

Ten years later, it is still three steps forward and two back, but we're making progress. God has never again spoken to me through a dream, but I am not dismissive of others' 'pictures', visions', and 'dreams'. I might not have married Alison but for that one dream.

Dreams, visions and angels

The prophets laid claim to frequent inspiration through visions by day and dreams by night. Numbers 12:6 establishes the principle, and Isaiah 6, Ezekiel 12:8, Daniel 7:1 and Zechariah 1:8 demonstrate the practice. Only on rare occasions were angels sent to prophets. 2 Kings 1:3–15, 1 Chronicles 21:18, Daniel 9:21 and Zechariah 1:9 are the only recorded incidents.

How did they prophesy?

Their speech

Though all the Old Testament prophets were inspired by the same God, each had a distinctive style. Isaiah is as different from Ezekiel as Rembrandt is from Picasso. The words were God's, but also man's. The prophets made no pretence about this, they knew they were only his mouth-pieces. They merely passed on the revelation they had received. But revelation is not dictation. They stamped their own personality on the prophecy and spoke it out in a great variety of styles. Narrative verse, prose, parables, direct speech, satire, psalms, laments, sermons, diatribe, midrash, all these, and more, are used. When they spoke they did not express an opinion, but brought an utterance which altered the situation. Prophecy is closely allied to blessing and cursing. What they announced—happened. Isaiah 40:6–8 and Isaiah 55:11 reveal the awesome power of the prophetic spoken word.

Their lives

The prophet's life was a prophecy. Hosea's unhappy marriage was a symbol. Jeremiah's life was a lesson. Ezekiel was a sign to the house of Israel, and Isaiah and his offspring were signs and portents. The way they lived proclaimed a message of justice and reconciliation equally as powerfully as their words, they were not called 'men of God' for nothing (see Isaiah 8:18; Jeremiah 16; Ezekiel 4:3; 12:6, 11; 24:24; Hosea 1:3).

Their actions

Some prophets used symbolic, dramatic acts as part of their prophesying. These were not visual aids but prophetic deeds which, in their own right, proclaimed what God had said and thought. Exodus 17:9, Jeremiah 19:1, 10, 11, and Ezekiel 4:1–3 are examples. Other prophets used miracles. In fact, the only Old Testament miracle workers were the prophets. Moses, Elijah and Elisha are obvious examples, but see also 1 Kings 13:1–10.

How were they distinguished from false prophets?

There was no test to establish a false prophecy, only to sift out the false prophets. Moses gave two guides in Deuteronomy 13:1–5 and Deuteronomy 18:21–22.
(i)   The failure of their predictive prophecies (although the corollary is not necessarily true: fulfilment is not a proof of genuineness).
(ii)   They call people after gods other than the one true God.
     Jeremiah and Ezekiel offered further tests in Jeremiah 23:9–40 and Ezekiel 12:21–14:11.
     These tests are similar to each other:
(i)   Their lifestyles are immoral.
(ii)   They do not check immorality in others, whereas a true prophet calls people to holiness.
(iii) They call for peace with no regard to the moral and spiritual conditions required for peace.
     We will add Jesus' test to these guidelines in an examination of prophecy today.

Old Testament prophecy is the essential foundation upon which any understanding of prophecy must be built. The weakness of much contemporary charismatic prophesying can be traced to an incomplete awareness of the Old Testament principles which should undergird prophecy. We will refer back to these basic Old Testament ideas as we attempt to establish a cohesive picture of God's intentions for prophecy in the years remaining before the Second Advent.

Prophets and Prophecy in the New Testament

Prophecy

The New Testament introduces a new age and a new organization for prophecy. It retains the basic Old Testament understanding, but the church, rather than isolated individuals, is the centre of prophetic activity; and prophetic activity is central to the church. Revelation 11:3–13 suggests that prophecy should be on the world's main stage throughout history. Three and a half years is a biblical symbol for persecution. I believe it refers here to the period of time from the Ascension to Armageddon. Prophecy is one of God's priorities in this era. The number 'two', a biblical symbol for witness, is a key word in this passage. Prophecy, like evangelism, is best described as an act of witness, and, because of the number two, as a corporate activity.

The two lamps refer to Moses and Elijah, the witnesses of the transfiguration. They are the supreme examples of 'word' and 'Spirit' inspired prophecy. These two facets of prophecy straddle the years. The two olive trees symbolize Joshua and Zerubbabel in the book of Zechariah. Joshua was the religious leader and Zerubbabel the civil leader of the repatriated community who restored the city and the Temple after the Exile. Prophecy should be directed to both the religious and the civil areas of life, not just the church. The two types of prophet should work together in the two parallel realms of prophecy. Some have made a very good case for 'word' inspired prophets functioning in society and 'Spirit' inspired prophets focusing on the church, but it should not be overstressed. Joshua and Zerubbabel were the two leaders who built the new Temple, and nothing builds the church like prophecy. As will be seen later, the main thrust of the gift of prophecy is to build together and build up the church. Ephesians 2:20, in teaching that the prophets were part of the foundation of the building which is the church, merely prefigures Revelation 11.

Numbers 11:16–17, 24–30 is the story of Moses in need of help, but his prophetic burden could only be shared with those on whom the Spirit came. This was restricted to the seventy elders. When Joshua queried Eldad and Medad's prophesying, an exasperated Moses answered him with an unintended prophetic prayer which has rung through the ages: 'If only the whole people of Yahweh were prophets, and Yahweh gave his Spirit to them all!' God heard and honoured that prayer, and Joel, in 2:28–29, foretold the day when God would do just this. God kept his promise at Pentecost when he poured out his Spirit without restriction upon the church. Peter, in quoting these words in Acts 2:18, added the important phrase, 'and they will prophesy' (see NIV). Since Pentecost, the possibility of prophesying has been open to all in the church who have been filled with Holy Spirit. On the day of Pentecost, there was no limitation on the giving of the Spirit and no restriction on the receiving. Potentially, all the church, without any distinction between male or female, old or young, lay or ordained, can prophesy.

When Peter spoke those words about prophecy, he

surely understood them as meaning that the whole church would perpetuate and expand the ministry of the Old Testament prophets. The whole people of God could now be men of God; servants of God; called and calling, seen and seeing; all could now enter into the presence of the Holy God and hear his secrets; all could pass on God's thoughts about reconciliation, social justice and national events; all could predict and proclaim; all intercede; all could be inspired by the 'word' and the 'Spirit'; all could receive dreams and visions; all speak, live and work miracles as the prophets of old.

The promise was not that all would be prophets, but that all could prophesy. This is an important distinction. The prophesying of the early church is clearly seen in the everyday behaviour of the saints in the book of Acts, but there still remained those called prophets. It is the same in other areas of ministry. All are commissioned to evangelize, but not all are evangelists; all are commanded to heal, but not all are healers; all are called to teach, but not all are teachers. The only exception is in deliverance. All believers are instructed and equipped to cast out demons, but there is no biblical élite set apart for this ministry. How topsy-turvy things have become!

The New Testament stresses that prophecy is part of the witness of the church. *Marturia*—witness, not *kerugma*—preaching, is meant to be the church's main 'outreach' activity. Revelation 19:10 amplifies this. It states, not that all prophecy should be just a witness, but that prophecy should be the same witness that Jesus gave. Jesus' witness was to the name and glory of God. Prophecy must point men to God as Jesus pointed men to God. Prophecy should focus on what God is doing, thinking and saying, not on a human response. Simply put, the essential New Testament prophetic message to the Jews was, 'God is angry with you because you have rejected and crucified the Messiah.' It pointed to God and his

A Prophecy to one Eastbourne Church

The following prophecy was given to the leaders of a growing church on December 24th 1981. It was brought by one who is to me the clearest example in East Sussex of one who exercises the ministry of prophet. He is a surveyor by trade.

'As you look back you see the fulfilment of my words to you as a fellowship, and as you look forward into 1982 many anticipations are in your hearts. I shall continue to build my kingdom of love and power among you irrespective of the setting of your fellowship, for my promise is to you as a people—not to a denomination.

'You will come out of your denomination at the point where your Council attempts to halt the growing work of my Spirit among you. It will be at this point that each of your members will be faced with the choice of whether to continue in the building that I am constructing. It will be a difficult choice for some, and you should pray now that none will choose wrongly out of fear or uncertainty; for there are many who will know in their innermost being what they should do, but will be intimidated by fear.

'I announce this beforehand so that when it occurs you who are leaders should not be desperate in any way, but know that I, the Lord, am at work accomplishing the building work that I have promised. My arms are open to all my children. I will not willingly exclude any from the new life that I am pouring into my body, and it is only when people stubbornly and persistently resist that division occurs. Some people may choose to exclude themselves from the richness of my blessing, but my mercy will never depart from any of my children.'

In June 1982, the trustees of their small denomination requested that the vast majority of the congregation should leave. It was the most amicable 'split' I have ever encountered.

anger, not to the Jews. Prophecy should bring the fear of God into a situation. It often announces bad news. Only when the human response to the prophesying is, 'Then what can I do to be saved?' can evangelism effectively take place; and this, not prophecy, points to the human response. The New Testament church knew that prophecy had to precede evangelism. It was the secret of their success. Most contemporary evangelists need to re-learn this lesson. Evangelism which is not preceded by the prophetic act of pointing to God's thoughts about the situation or person, is a waste of time and money.

Those who purport to be opposed to prophecy usually attempt to base their opposition on the importance of Scripture as the eternal unalterable word. They consider that prophecy must be either tautological or evil. I find it strange that all the teaching about prophecy is taken from the very book they seek to defend. 2 Timothy 3:16 teaches that all Scripture is 'God-breathed'—expired rather than inspired. Scripture has a unique authority which can never be equalled. Scripture is for all people, at all times, in all places, whereas prophecy is for a particular person, in a particular place, at a particular time. The New Testament church often used the phrase 'the Law and the Prophets' to describe the double-bladed word of the Old Testament revelation. That principle continued and continues. Prophecy must not add to, nor differ from, Scripture, but is its essential, immediate supplement and application. 2 Peter 1:19 is unequivocal, 'You will be right to depend on prophecy and take it as a lamp for lighting a way through the dark until the dawn comes and the morning star rises in your minds.' This 'until', and the reference in 1 Corinthians 13:8–9 to the disappearance of imperfection, has led some to conclude, mistakenly, that prophecy ceased with the completion of the canon of Scripture. This idea would force us to the two incredible and nonsensical conclusions that, firstly, we must live in an age when all knowledge has long since ceased and, secondly, we are no different from Jehovah's Witnesses as we believe that the Day of the Lord has dawned, the Morning Star has come, perfection is here and we see Christ face to face. I find it far easier to believe that prophecy is still for today!

The New Testament reminds us that the Old Testament prophets were rejected and persecuted, and it promises this as the lot of all who will prophesy. Matthew 5:11–12 and Luke 11:49 show this in part, but it is more fully developed in Revelation. Revelation 6:9 shows the large number of saints killed for prophesying, and 12:17 reveals the extreme opposition of the dragon to those who obey God and bear witness—which includes prophesying—for Jesus.

Prophets

The New Testament prophets were one of Christ's special gifts to the church after his ascension (Ephesians 4:7–16). They were given to help build up the church. This function of prophets is normally linked in the New Testament to the 'gift of prophecy'—see pages 47-56. The prophets were not elected by the church, nor chosen by the elders, but were those men or women whom the church recognized as regularly receiving and delivering prophecies from God. They were simply those who prophesied more frequently than the rest.

The prophets normally occupy the second place after the apostles. Ephesians 2:20 suggests this is because of their place as part of the church's foundation. Ephesians 3:5 reveals that they are part of the church's foundation because, along with the apostles, it is their task to reveal the mystery, unknown to previous generations, that the pagans were to share in the inheritance of Israel. Every time a new local church is begun in an area where the gospel has not previously been proclaimed it is necessary to have prophets who will repeat this foundational task.

Acts 13:1–3 presents the Antioch prophets at worship when they were charged by the Holy Spirit with consecrating Barnabas and Saul to a task which he had already revealed to them. Their inward call was now confirmed by the prophets' outward call. Just as the Old Testament prophets anointed the kings and set them apart for ruling, so the New Testament prophets laid hands on the ministers and consecrated them for serving. 1 Timothy 1:18 and 4:14, and 2 Timothy 1:6 illustrate this function which was reserved for the prophets.

In Acts 21:10–14, we read how Agabus, the best known prophet of the early church, visited Paul, and with both a prophetic action and prophetic speech, warned Paul of what was to take place, so that he could be prepared. The prophecy was not to prevent Paul from going to Jerusalem, but to warn him of what would happen. This advance knowledge meant that when the riot began (verse 30) Paul was prepared and could be sure of the hand of God in the matter. His longed-for journey to Rome was under way at last.

Agabus also echoed the cries for social justice of his prophetic forebears when he revealed the Spirit's great interest in famine relief (Acts 11:27–30). Stirred by the Spirit, Agabus predicted the great famine of A.D. 49–50 which swept westwards through the Roman empire. This enabled the church to make adequate preparation. Agabus pointed only to what God was doing. There was no demand for human response in the prophecy, no injunction to take up a collection, just a warning to prepare for a coming famine. This, with its echo of Genesis 41, is real famine relief: to provide before the shortage occurs.

No study of New Testament prophets or prophecy could be complete without looking at the Prophet of the Bible, the Prophet who is mighty in word and deed. Jesus is the prophet par excellence, and to him we now turn.

Jesus the Supreme Prophet

In Deuteronomy 18:15–20 we read how Moses prepared the people for the leadership of Joshua, but also prophesied that God would send another prophet like himself. At the time of Christ, the Jews expected the coming Messiah to be another Moses; another prophet to whom God would reveal himself as in Numbers 12:6–8; who would repeat, on a grand scale, the prodigies of the Exodus. When the priests and Levites questioned John the Baptist, in John 1:19–25, they wanted to establish if he were 'the Prophet'. Peter, in Acts 3:22–24, shows that he believed Christ to be this Prophet.

Time and again, Jesus was recognized by the people as a prophet. Cleopas, in Luke 24:19, understood Jesus to be a prophet by the things he said and did. The Samaritan woman at Jacob's well realized that Jesus was a prophet when the Spirit informed him how many husbands she had had (John 4:18). The crowds received him as the Prophet when he fed the five thousand (John 6:14) and rode into Jerusalem on the donkey (Matthew 21:11). Christ's enemies referred to him as a prophet in the dispute with Nicodemus (John 7:52) and in Matthew 13:57 Jesus himself seemed to consider himself to be a prophet.

Rev. John Bickersteth—St Peter's, Ashburnham, E. Sussex

Late in the 1960s, John Bickersteth, the vicar of Ashburnham and leader of the Conference centre at Ashburnham Place, was invited to a meeting in Bexhill to be addressed by a schoolmaster from Kenya, Mr Godfrey Dawkins. John had to leave before the end of the after-meeting, so did not meet Mr Dawkins personally that evening.

However, it was mentioned to Godfrey that a John Bickersteth of Ashburnham Place had been at the meeting. He immediately remembered a photograph of Ashburnham Place which he had seen in a Christian magazine. As Godfrey had looked at this, the Lord had given him a two-fold message for the leader of that centre. Firstly, that he was not to specialize in deliverance from occult bondage, but rather to continue a balanced ministry; and secondly, that bringing the renewal to English people of aristocratic background should be a priority.

Godfrey immediately resolved to visit Ashburnham Place the following day to deliver this prophetic message to John. When he arrived, he could not possibly have known that John was praying that very week about how far he should specialize in the work of deliverance, nor that John was the Chairman of an association of twenty-five Bible Study groups in London specially set up to try and help those of 'upper class' backgrounds who were just then encountering renewal for the first time.

Godfrey Dawkins' prophecy to John Bickersteth confirmed John's personal guidance; it helped to influence the acceptance of renewal by the aristocratic members of the Bible Study groups, and indelibly validated for John the idea that God wishes to use prophecy today. John went on from this earnestly to desire the gift of prophecy, and has himself been used considerably by God in a similar fashion for the last fifteen years.

Right through his ministry, Christ manifested all the signs of an extraordinary prophet. Prophets were close to the Father's heart, but John 1:18 shows that Jesus was nearest of all to the Father's heart. Prophets are those who share God's secrets, but Matthew 11:27 suggests a degree of intimacy unparalleled even by Moses. Jesus knew and revealed the Father perfectly. The Gospel of John reveals Jesus as one totally under his Father's authority. Jesus never went anywhere, did anything, spoke or acted except in obedient response to an initiative from his Father. John's Gospel shows Jesus as the 'sent' one. This is close to the Old Testament pattern of a divine commission following the whispering of secrets into the prophet's ear. Jesus was sent to a clearly delineated area (Matthew 15:24) with a unique prophetic calling. He was to prophesy to a certain people in a particular place for a limited period of time. The sudden appearing and commencement of prophetic activity seen in Elijah and Amos is repeated in Christ. One day he was a private repairer of chairs whom nobody noticed as being at all unusual. Then he was sent. Six weeks later he was mending bodies and prophesying with an authority which astonished all who heard him.

His words were the spoken words of God. Prophets are God's mouthpiece. They announce his thoughts. Jesus, in John 12:49–50, claimed no originality for his speech. Everything he spoke was what the Father had told him. But Jesus was not all talk and no action. He was the Prophet 'mighty in word and deed'. His words were confirmed by his deeds. Some sections of the church have so defended his deity as to dehumanize him but he was fully God and fully man. Their defence of his deity has given the impression that Jesus worked miracles because he was God. This is not so. It would make a hollow mockery of his promises for 'greater things' and 'signs following' to those who believe in him. Jesus performed miracles because he was a man full of the Spirit of God. The Old Testament prophets worked wonders only because they had been anointed with the Spirit. Jesus did the same. The miraculous is accessible to all recipients of the Spirit. The entertaining blind beggar of John 9 identified Jesus as a prophet because Jesus had opened his eyes.

The Old Testament identification of the Spirit with prophecy is brought to a climax in Jesus. Peter, in his talk at the house of Cornelius, quoted Isaiah 61:1 and applied it to Jesus: 'God has anointed him with the Holy Spirit and with power, and because God was with him'—not because he was God—'Jesus went about doing good and curing all who had fallen into the power of the devil' (Acts 10:38). Jesus' baptism was the pivotal point of his thirty-eight years. As he rose from the river, the sky was split and the Spirit came down. In that moment Jesus became *Christos* —the anointed. He was set apart as a beloved Spirit-anointed prophet.

His predecessors announced and anointed kings and other prophets. John the Baptist introduced Jesus (and this is so vital that it is included in each Gospel) as the one who would baptize in Holy Spirit. Jesus' first essential prophetic ascended activity was to anoint his bride with Holy Spirit, to set the church apart as a race of prophets, priests and kings. His second prophetic act (and this will continue until he comes) was, and is, to intercede at the Father's right hand for the saints. Jesus followed in the ministerial footsteps of his prophetic ancestors in every possible way. He was even crucified as a false prophet. He abandoned his policy of messianic secrecy by acknowledging that he was the Messiah, and then went further by revealing himself as the Lord of Psalm 110 and the mysterious personage of heavenly origin in Daniel 7:13 (Matthew 26:64–68). The Sanhedrin's response to his bold claim was to brand him a false prophet and call for his death.

Jesus was even a true prophet in a predictive sense. Luke 21:20–24 was spoken in about A.D. 33. In A.D. 70 Titus surrounded Jerusalem. The Christians, remembering this prophecy, evacuated the city and were guided to Pella. No Christians were captured or killed in the ensuing massacre. This accuracy should give us great confidence that his other prophecy, given at the same moment, will also be fulfilled. Luke 21:25–28 is longed for, prayed for, and awaited with eager anticipation.

Most false religions acknowledge Jesus as a prophet. It is probably due to this that such scant attention is paid to his prophetic status by the evangelical sector of the church. Yet Jesus was much more than just another prophet. His birth, life, ministry, death, resurrection, ascension and activity at Pentecost confirmed all that the Old Testament prophets had foretold. 'It is to him that all the prophets bear witness' (Acts 10:43). Over three hundred detailed prophecies were fulfilled in his life. This is amazing. A prophet can do no more than speak or demonstrate the word of God, but Jesus was the Word incarnate. Acts 10:43 tells us that all the prophets before Jesus bore witness to him. Revelation 19:10 instructs that all prophecy should be operated by the Spirit of Jesus and must bear testimony to him. Jesus is the supreme prophet, and all others who prophesy must point to him. He is both our example in prophesying and the object of our prophesying.

The Prophetic Church Today

We have looked briefly at biblical prophecy. I now turn to the application of the principles we have unearthed. Firstly, I will paint a broad canvas to show a wide view of the church as a prophetic community. Then we will look in detail at the function of prophecy in building up the church and building it together. Finally, I will make some suggestions on how we can move from where we are to where we ought to be. It is a difficult journey, some of the path has not been trodden for a very long time.

When Peter announced the arrival of the day prophesied long ago by Joel, he understood it to mean that, henceforth, all the church—every single believer—could, and should, engage in the activity of the Old Testament prophets. Today, the whole church should announce what once was the privilege of a few. In one sense, the very existence of the Christian community is a prophetic sign of the kingdom of God to the world; in the same way, the lives of the Old Testament prophets and their families spoke clearly to the people amongst whom they lived. The church is meant to be both evangelistic and prophetic, without being exclusively one or the other. The two are the opposite faces of the coin we call 'witness'. Evangelism

St Mary's, Barcombe, E. Sussex

On Thursday, May 9th 1985, seven people from this small rural Anglican church met for the weekly Thursday afternoon prayer time. As is their habit, they began their two-hour meeting by seeking guidance from God as to what and whom they should pray for.

One member of the group had the distinct impression that they should pray for Graham Tomsett, a church member whose wife was present at this prayer group. As they began to pray for Graham, another in the group experienced a sudden, extraordinary sense of overwhelming tiredness and weariness (and they had only just started praying!). She mentioned this to the others and they took this to mean that Graham, himself, was very tired. Jacky, Graham's wife, said that he had been working away for several weeks, only returning home at weekends, and was exhausted.

As they prayed on for Graham, one lady received the thought that they should urge Graham to take a holiday, then another saw the date 'June 3rd' in her mind's eye, and another visualized a detailed picture of a cottage with a field beyond. Jacky mentioned all of this to Graham that weekend and discovered that his work away would be completed on Friday, May 31st; so he booked himself out of work for the week beginning Monday, June 3rd.

Meanwhile, one of the prayer group had found an available cottage in South Molton, Devon, another had paid the rent and another volunteered to have their three children for the week. When Graham and Jacky arrived at Primrose Cottage, they discovered it exactly matched the details given in the prophetic picture. They had a glorious week's holiday, their first alone in their entire life. This would never have happened if this small country church had not taken prophecy seriously.

proclaims the offer of forgiveness, freedom, a future and
a new family. Prophecy promises that, even if this is
rejected, Sovereign God will have his way; he will establish
his kingdom in righteousness and judgement. Evangelism
and prophecy cannot be separated without making both
null and void. Prophecy without evangelism will only lead
to frustration, despair and humanism. Evangelism without
prophecy is a grim, soul-breaking slog with little fruit.

Witness is an important and large topic for study. It has
many different parts. These include incarnational living,
prophecy, evangelistic proclamation, confirming signs and
wonders, persuasion, regeneration and baptism. These
should be empowered by the Spirit to give glory to God
and build the church. Though we will now lift prophecy
out for close examination, its place and inter-relationships
with the other facets of witness must never be forgotten.

The Sermon on the Mount is Christ's manifesto of his
kingdom. In this sermon, Christ used 'salt' and 'light' as
two prophetic pictures. They are his marks of the kingdom. He used another picture in the commissioning of the
seventy-two: 'lambs among wolves'. I believe that these
three pictures give an overview of Christ's expectation for
his prophetic church.

Salt

The phrase 'the salt of the world' shows a prophetic
function for the church in purification. Today we use salt
mainly for flavouring, but the ancients used it both to
preserve from decay and to purify that which had decayed.
Leviticus 2:13, 2 Kings 2:20 and Ezekiel 16:4 show this.
Salt was a predecessor of Elsan fluid. 'You are the Elsan
fluid of the world' brings the picture up to date for those
who are campers. The church has this twin prophetic
function of preserving society from decay and purifying
that which has already decayed. Can this function ever
have been more urgently needed than it is today?

Light

The expression 'the light of the world' suggests that the church should be a means of illumination and revelation. The church should live in obedience to the word of God and bring the light of the word to shine on society, and reveal the true nature of its problems. The Old Testament prophets prophesied when the word of the Lord came to them. Our acceptance of and corporate obedience to the word should lead to a prophetic revelation of it to the world.

Lambs among wolves

This prophetic illustration indicates the need for the prophetic people to live out their 'servant' nature. The prophet mighty in word and deed was the Lamb. His flock enters and lives in his kingdom by the same 'lamb' principle of self-sacrifice and service. Everybody in the world wants to be a 'wolf'. No one wants to lie down and be a 'lamb'. It is essential that the church and individual Christians should take care not to dominate others. We are called to accept the domination of others and daily offer our lives as a sacrifice pleasing to God—united with the sacrifice of Jesus. We must accept that we have to be 'fleeced' before we can be glorified. I suggest the following ways in which the church should fulfil its prophetic calling in the world today.

Reconciliation

The Old Testament prophets held this as central. Jesus was the reconciler. The church will only be prophetic when reconciliation is a visible feature of its life and message. Our reconciliation with God must be demonstrated by genuine reconciliation within the church, in each local congregation, and by a continuing message of reconciliation to, and in, the world. This is of supreme importance: in the family, between spouses and between parents and children; in the workplace, between employer and employee; in society, between black and white, rich and poor, north and south, employed and unemployed, landlord and tenant. Unholy divisions in the body of Christ deny the message and must be called sin. Alienation and discord within the church need to be identified and rectified so that the church can be this reconciled community. As the judgement of God is poured out upon society, the prophetic church needs to shout, 'Get right with God and get right with each other.' We must consciously see ourselves as, and become, a 'counter-culture'.

Social justice

The Old Testament prophets worked, lived and prophesied for justice in society. The poor, the widows and strangers were all to be cared for. They announced God's curse upon those who were apathetic to the poor and his blessing upon those who made generous provision. This was echoed in the early church, and should be today. The Christian community has a particular responsibility for the poor and oppressed. We are called to defend the cause of the needy within our nation and world. This will not result in popularity, but in persecution. Matthew 25:31–46 is not yet taken seriously. A prophetic church should clearly articulate God's thoughts, not her own ideas, about the greed-riddled capitalistic system we exist in. Those, like Bishop Tutu, with the office of prophet, speaking out for justice in places like Southern Africa, and others in our inner cities, need support and prayer, not carping criticism because of theological differences. The Bishop of Durham may seem doctrinally bankrupt, but he was like a true prophet in his pleas for reconciliation and social justice during the 1984/85 miners' strike.

National issues

The prophets of old were frequently summoned by their kings to reveal God's thoughts about the events and issues of the day. We too need to pass on God's thoughts about contemporary issues. We should be asking prayerful questions like, 'What does God hate most in our society?'; 'What does God think about embryo experimentation?'; 'How does God react to the opening of a Buddhist Temple by the official head of the Church of England?' The church must prophetically address such issues. When the church has done this in the past, revival has followed. It is the old principle of prophecy making evangelism effective. One example is those early nineteenth century American churches which stood out and spoke out against slavery, even when it was highly respectable. They were the ones who enjoyed revival; God did not send this blessing to any slave-owning churches. Every revival, from monasticism to the present day, has been preceded by several common factors. One of these has been the prophetic announcement of God's anger at a particular national issue. This has varied from the mistreatment of serfs, prisoners or slaves, to prostitution, drunkenness and child labour. I believe that our key issue today is abortion.

Real enemy

Monotheism should be the monotonous cry of all true prophets. This involves pointing out the real enemy, so that the church and the nation are not distracted by religious, economic or sociological red herrings. The Bible reveals two enemies: Satan and death. We are called to the difficult task of prophetically pointing people away from these enemies. Satan is always suggesting false enemies. The church, in different places and at different times, has fought Turks, Jews, Anabaptists, Negroes, Nazis, Commmunists, Capitalists, Catholics, Charismatics, etc, etc: an endless list of opponents, which the church has fought with Satan's tactics and weapons. A prophetic church needs to listen carefully to God to see how Satan is working today and then to expose his intrigues. The Enemy behind the enemy must be seen in order to avoid false remedies which only exacerbate the problem. Those who see the enemy as Communism or Capitalism tend to back its economic or political opposite as the remedy. This was not Christ's way. I suggest that two contemporary guises of the enemy are freemasonry and spiritism. One attracts men, the other, women. Both have stifled and restricted the renewal and growth of the church. Where is the prophetic church which will plead for mercy upon Harold Devereux-Still and Doris Stokes? Who will clearly expose the Evil One behind these foul practices? When will the church proclaim that these and other organizations and ideas are evil, that they are where the Enemy is working? We must applaud the Methodist Conference for taking the stand it has and pray that other denominations will follow in their footsteps.

Servanthood

The church will be truly prophetic only when servanthood becomes central to its way of life. Biblical prophets were servants. Jesus came to serve and illustrated this by washing feet. Matthew 20:20–28 and 23:1–12 merit close study and application. Understanding without obedience is blasphemy. If the church is to be prophetic, its love of power, position and status must be eradicated. The greatness of a Christian is measured by how well and often he washes feet. The world's leaders exercise authority. This should not be so in the church. Here the leaders should serve, as Mother Teresa serves. Jesus does not advocate humility in office. He rejects office. Clericalism is the blight of the church, both in the traditional denominations and in the new Restoration denominations. One emphasizes appearance, the other, authority. Neither stresses lowly service. How does wearing the hood of our degree, or having our name printed in large letters on publicity, help in lowly service? Jesus' words in Matthew 23:8–12 are the great indictment of our age. The world has been hoodwinked into believing that the world can only be changed by politics and political weapons. This view must be rejected. The church's weapons are truth, not advertising; righteousness and justice, not violence; peace-filled submission, not a power struggle; faith, not ideology; salvation, not utopianism; the word of God, not satellite television; prayer, not effective actions. The church must be weak and vulnerable, so that the strength and power of God can be revealed. This is the way of the poor man from Galilee.

Intercession

The prophets of old were the intercessors of their day. If the church is to be prophetic, then intercession must come centre stage again. God's Spirit has caused thousands of church prayer meetings to close in the last twenty years. This is because he is ushering in a new age and understanding of intercession. New wine needs new wineskins. The only historic sign of revival in the 1984 multi-million pound Mission England saga was the Prayer Triplet scheme. If the scheme continues and grows it will be a real part of the new era of intercession, which will prepare the highway for the coming King. (The *Ashburnham Insight* book on intercession makes several suggestions on how to intercede, how not to intercede, and what to expect from intercession.) If the church cares enough to prophesy, it must care enough to pray.

The church as a whole, every local expression and each individual member, should prophesy about all these matters to their friends, neighbours and workmates, but God will, from time to time, raise up those called to the office of prophet, to address these matters in a particularly public and costly manner. I have already suggested some names. Such people need our unswerving support, care and prayers. Desmond Tutu and Mary Whitehouse did not decide to become prophets. God alone raised them up. It should be our fervent prayer that God will raise up an increasing number of true prophets, and that the church be given the discernment to detect the inevitable false prophets.

As the end of the age draws near, prophecy will become a crucial issue and it will be vital to establish the line between true and false. The Old Testament tests still apply. Jesus added his principle in Matthew 7:15–20. We are not to judge by superficial appearance, but by the effect, the fruit, of the person's ministry and life. The principles seen in Acts 10:43 and Revelation 19:10 are crucial. All true prophets and prophecy will point to Jesus, to his life and work. Any purported prophet who does not witness that those who believe in Jesus have their sins forgiven through his name, who does not witness as Jesus witnessed, can safely be rejected.

The Gift of Prophecy

One of the cries of the Old Testament was that the day would come when all the Lord's people—and not just the select few—would prophesy. This came about when Christ baptized the church in Holy Spirit at Pentecost. The church entered into a new era to be characterized by prophecy. We are meant to reveal to society God's thoughts and his actions, to be bearers of bad news. One of the chief reasons for the failure of contemporary evangelism is that the message is not construed as good news. 'You can be saved' brings no delight to the person who does not realize he needs to be saved. That person needs to be exposed to God's thoughts. Prophecy brings the fear of God into a situation. It calls people to get right with God. It announces the arrival of the judgement of God. It calls nations to social justice. It points out the true enemy. Our ministry must be both prophetic—'This is what God thinks about you', and evangelistic—'This is what God has done to bring a change'. Our lives should show the fear of God and the joy of the Lord. Fear brings revelation. Joy gives strength.

The gift of prophecy is quite different. It is a separate sub-heading within the giant subject of prophecy.

47

Prophecy is primarily to the world, whereas the gift of prophecy is God's private means of communication with his beloved church. It is that part of prophecy which is given during public worship. It is not the sum total of prophecy, but it is a significant part of it. Charismatics are right to emphasize this gift, but not to the exclusion of wider prophecy. Those groups which decry this gift fly in the face of Scripture. The last twenty-five years have brought a general acceptance of the possibility of the present-day reality of the gifts listed in 1 Corinthians 12, but their usage is still embryonic. We are in uncharted waters. Few can speak with authority; therefore what follows is both tentative and experimental. I have many questions and few answers, but some stimuli are needed to move the thinking and practice of this gift forward from the stale, out-dated stereotypes which abound today. The Ashburnham Stable Family is attempting to implement the following suggestions, but is finding it hard to move from tradition to truth!

1 Corinthians 11–15 is about the church public worship, especially the Eucharist, the Lord's Supper. It is incorrect to find individual or counselling applications in these chapters. The key Greek verb of chapter 14 is *oikodomeo*. This is often translated as 'to edify'. It means 'to build together in order to build up'. If we desire the church of which we are a part to be built together and built up, special attention must be paid to this chapter. The following 21 lessons about the gift of 'prophecy' and its companion gift of 'separation' are drawn from 1 Corinthians chapter 14.

1. Our churches are called to *zeloo* for prophecy (verse 1). This is a strong verb meaning 'to have great zeal', or 'to crave'. Love must be our main ambition, with prophecy a close second. Our corporate prayers should regularly include passionate heartfelt petitions for the gift of prophecy. Most groups pray for the Queen more often

than they do for prophecy! This precious gift will only become more common and fully developed when the church obeys this command to crave for prophecy. We need to show God that we are serious about wanting him to speak to us.

2. A prophecy is a message from God to men (verse 3). It is vital for the church to distinguish between *diermeneuo*, 'to explain a tongue' and *propheteuo* 'to prophesy'. Some still offer the stale and hoary equation, tongues + explanation = prophecy. This is not so. Verse 5 shows that tongues plus explanation is of equivalent value to prophecy, but it is not the equivalent of prophecy. Both build the church, but verses 2 and 3 show that they do this from opposite directions. Verse 2 is unambiguous. The direction of tongues and explanation is prayer or praise from man to God. The direction of prophecy is revelation from God to man. The common charismatic practice is for a tongue to remain unexplained with a subsequent prophecy being deemed the explanation. This is a misordering of both tongues and prophecy. (This topic has been dealt with in some detail in the Ashburnham Insight book *Tongues and Explanations*.)

3. A prophecy can be *oikodome*. This means that its content will show how God wants to build us together to build us up (verse 3).

4. Or it can be a *paraklesis*. This means that its content will reveal what God is doing and will call us to fall in step with this, to come alongside God in what he is doing. It is closely related to *parakletos*, the revealed name of the Holy Spirit. Its usual rendering of encouragement or consolation is misleading. Its derivation is from *para*, 'by the side' and *kaleo*, 'to call'. A *paraklesis* is not God saying, 'You are a nice group of people,' but rather, 'I am opposed to the occult shop in North Street. I mean to remove it. Come alongside me as I do this. Join with me in this action' (verse 3).

Battle Baptist Church, E. Sussex

When Dennis Nolan was appointed part-time pastor of this country church in 1980, it had twenty-three members. Dennis had been filled with Holy Spirit in 1969 and so, prayerfully, he sought to encourage his tiny congregation into seeking the gifts of God's Spirit. Gradually this happened and during 1981 the first prophecy was offered in a Sunday service. From 1981 to 1983 a number of encouraging prophecies were brought, many by visitors who knew nothing of the larger pattern.

By the autumn of 1983, the membership had risen to thirty-seven, but few Battle residents had been converted. The growth was mainly through transfer and a few conversions in outlying villages. God gave a prayer burden for effectiveness and boldness in reaching the local people and, in October 1983, two praying ladies felt a sudden urge to visit a local street, Mount Joy. They went, prayed and wrestled with the forces of darkness and mentioned all this to nobody.

Carol singing evenings were planned towards Christmas, and on Friday, December 16th, arrangements were made to visit Wellington Gardens, some three hundred yards from the church. At the brief prayer time before they set out, Dennis's wife, Pat, had strange words come to mind. She said, 'Cast your nets on the right hand side of the ship.' After pondering, the carol singers changed their plans and decided to visit the street immediately to the right of the church, Mount Joy.

Meanwhile, at 23 Mount Joy, a small boy was pestering his parents to go carol singing. When they heard the singing outside, the dad, an accountant, asked if his son could join in for the evening. Out of that brief contact, the boy, his parents and his grandparents, went to church the following Sunday evening for the first time.

In eight weeks his parents were saved. Within nine months, five adults from that one family were converted. Since then, they have all been baptized and filled with Holy Spirit, and another Mount Joy resident has been saved. One wonders what would have happened if the prophecy had been suppressed or ignored.

5. Or it can be a *paramuthia*. This means that its content is 'near speech'. It is God whispering a very tender message of love or comfort into the ear of his beloved Son's bride. This seems to be reserved for those churches undergoing persecution (verse 3).

6. The one who prophesies does not build himself up (as does the tongue-bringer) (verse 4). Those who exercise this gift often testify to a great emptiness and exhaustion after even the briefest sentence. Therefore it is our custom, though biblically unsubstantiated, always to bless those who have prophesied in a meeting or service.

7. The one who prophesies should build together and build up the church (verse 4 and verse 26). Those who speak 'knocking' prophecies should, like those who pray 'prayer sermons', be challenged and corrected.

8. The one who prophesies is of great importance (verse 5). We must not treat prophecy casually, but must give the respect due to those men and women to whom God has entrusted a particular message for that meeting.

9. We are to be *zelotes* for prophecy and explanation since these are two gifts which edify the church (verse 12). This is the second time in just a few verses that we are instructed to be zealous and eager, craving prophecy. It must be important.

10. I have no idea what verses 22–25 mean. (And it seems to me that neither have any of the commentators. They outdo each other in offering implausible suggestions.) Maybe I am just dull, but I cannot harmonize these verses with themselves and the rest of Paul's writings.

11. We are to be thoroughly prepared before the meeting (verse 26). All the members of the church should spend time in the week preparing themselves for the services, listening to God for the contributions he wishes them to make to the corporate worship. Any contribution—songs, talks, tongues, explanation or prophecies —can be given by the Spirit in advance. It is our custom for

people to telephone in their contribution, not so that the leader of the meeting can decide what to include, but so that he can, by the gift of wisdom, decide their order. Prophecies should not be submitted for 'testing' in advance, but should be submitted so that their correct place in the meeting can be established. (I have gone into this more fully in the Ashburnham Insight book *Tongues and Explanations*.)

12. A prophetic contribution may be an *apokalupsis* (verse 26). This will be the unveiling, the revealing, of something hitherto unknown. In the past we have spoken much of prophecy as the 'now' word of God. We ought also to talk about the 'new' word of God. New to us, not new to God; new to us as freshly unveiled, but utterly consistent with the nature and word of God as expressed in Scripture and right in line with the witness of Jesus.

13. Two or three prophecies should be brought (verse 29). The two or three of verse 27 is the maximum number of people who can bring tongues (there can be no more), though each can bring several. The two or three in this verse is a minimum (there can be no fewer). Isolated prophecies are highly questionable. After one prophecy the leader should wait until at least one other prophetic message has come before proceeding with the rest of the instructions in this verse.

14. After two, or definitely three, prophecies the leader must ensure that the 'others' spring into action (verse 29). Others is *allos* not *heteros* in Greek and, therefore, means those who habitually prophesy, but have not done so on this occasion. It is not for the clergy, elders, deacons or leaders privately to weigh, test, separate, sift, discern the prophecy, but only for those believers who regularly exercise this gift. It is quite wrong for churches to allow the minister or elders alone to test prophecy. It is the prerogative of the prophets, though any minister or elder who regularly prophesies would be part of such a group.

15. These 'others' do this, not by their experience, but by exercising the spiritual gift of the discerning of spirits, the gift of *diakrisis*. This means thorough judging, thorough discerning, or best of all, thorough separating. The traditional understanding is that the place of discernment is in exorcism. This must be questioned. The location of the gift here in 1 Corinthians 12 means that its primary use is public worship, not personal ministry. It is to prophecy what explanation is to tongues.

The number seven is usually of great significance in Scripture. It is a symbol of perfection. The seventh book in the Old Testament shows God's people in the promised land, clearing out the evil, under God's chosen leaders. It is all about judges and judging. The seventh section of the seventh book in the New Testament shows God's chosen people fulfilling God's purpose for them—worshipping him. The seventh gift in this section is all about judging and getting rid of evil. I find this most interesting. It is this gift of *diakrisis*. This word is used in Matthew 16:3 to show how a meaning can be derived from a picture; in 1 Corinthians 6:5 to establish the truth in a dispute; in 1 Corinthians 11:29–31 to show its crucial necessity; in 1 Corinthians 12:10 as the seventh gift; and in 1 Corinthians 14:29 to demonstrate its usage as the companion gift to prophecy. It is the gift which separates the divine message from the human dross which taints it.

The 'separators' listen to the two or three prophets and to the Spirit. They bear in mind the important principles that all activity of the Spirit points to Jesus and that prophecy shows what God is doing, thinking, saying rather than focusing on a human response. God in prophecy does not say, 'You do this,' but rather, 'This is what I am doing'. The emphasis is on the revelation of God, rather than any human response. The 'separators' do not give a thumbs up or a thumbs down to each individual prophecy, but separate that part influenced by evil spirits, that part

Sutton Coldfield Baptist Church, W. Midlands

On Saturday, November 7th 1981, Sutton Coldfield Baptist Church gathered for a day of prayer and fasting. Ten church leaders were to lead an hour each, culminating in a final act of worship. The purpose of the day was to seek specific direction from God for the future of the church, which was finding its premises both unsuitable and hopelessly overcrowded on Sundays and week nights.

The entire day produced no clear guidance, and the sense of anti-climax and disappointment was keenly felt by some. However, informal conversations revealed within a couple of days that at least two ladies, and possibly a couple more, had received clear pictures from the Lord about the church as a light, set on a literal hill, shining in the darkness, but that they felt these pictures appeared to have no practical application to current circumstances and so had not offered them publicly during the day.

In August 1982, two large school buildings, immediately across the road from the existing premises, were offered for sale by tender. They contained two and a half times the accommodation the church possessed at the time. They were situated high on a hill, and overlooked the whole town centre and main shopping centre of Sutton Coldfield. As soon as the buildings came up for offer, these prophetic pictures were recalled and the church felt it to be right to act upon them and attempt to purchase the nearby school properties. In a wonderful way the buildings were secured, and are now in use by the church. The validity of these prophetic pictures was clearly vindicated in a vivid way.

which is human enthusiasm and pass on from the several prophecies the common kernel, which is God's now or new word. It is not an exercise in comprehension and précis. It is a spiritual gift which operates in the same manner as tongues and prophecy.

This is most liberating. It eliminates the pastoral problems caused by rejection or fear of rebuff in the beginner, and is a glowing demonstration of the Body at work as a body. It is this separation of the prophecies which should be listened to, recorded and obeyed, not the individual prophecies. I suggest that after the prophecies have been brought, the recognized prophets, who did not prophesy, should quickly come together to wait upon God for the gift of separation. They can either do this while the meeting continues in their absence, or they can meet on the following day. When they have received the separation from God, they should announce it at an appropriate moment.

16. There is a place for both spontaneous and prepared prophecy. The norm is for the first prophecy to be prepared. The place for spontaneous prophecy is in interruption and confirmation (verse 30).

17. We must interrupt if a spontaneous prophecy is placed in our mind whilst another is being spoken (verse 30). There is an English repulsion at such behaviour, but it is a common legal practice and we only need re-educating for this to become seemly and orderly. Often the first two sentences of a prophecy are inspired, the next two are enthusiastic and the rest are feeble attempts to stop. An interruption by the next prophecy would greatly facilitate the separating.

18. For the third time, we must be *zelotes* for prophecy (verse 39). It must be very important. We should crave for prophecy much more than for signs and wonders. We should ache for God to speak in this way.

19. Prophecies must be brought with *euschemonos*

(verse 40). This means with beauty, or gracefully, not fortissimo, nor in archaic language, nor prefixed with 'Thus says the Lord', or 'Oh my children'! It is much better, in humility and with an awareness of our fallibility (1 Corinthians 13:9) and knowing the need for further prophecy and separation, to prefix to the prophecy the words, 'I think the Lord is suggesting something like . . . '.

20. They should be brought with a *taxis* (verse 40). This means with a deliberate arrangement, a drawing up in order. This is done by the leader with the help of the gift of wisdom.

21. This lovely gift is for everybody (verse 31). There may be several sets of two or three, each followed by a different separation. When churches start to be zealous for prophecy this will happen. Oh for that day to dawn! There will be problems, but I would rather have the problem of too many gifts, than the problem of too few.

This gift builds the church. If that be our heart's desire we will fall on our knees for this gift to *ginomai* (verse 40). Let prophecy, not 'be done', but rather 'become'—'come into being', 'happen'. We do not worship a dumb God. There is no gag in his mouth. We must extract the cotton wool from our ears which blocks out his voice.

Starting to Prophesy

It is a great tragedy that after twenty-five years of charismatic renewal there is still no place for regular prophecy. Very few Christians believe it is for today. The battle for the existence of tongues has, by and large, been won. The campaign for prophecy has not yet been so successful. There is a widespread fear of false prophets, but superficial prophecy is the main contemporary problem. We have a Christian leadership unprepared to make room for prophecy. They are still intellect-centred, analysis-orientated, rather than Spirit-hungry. Despite all the teaching there is little evidence of a developing community lifestyle. Only out of this will the body gifts flourish. Deacons, stewards and churchwardens have been re-christened elders, but few appreciate their function in protecting the church from, amongst other things, false prophets.

Satan is firmly opposed to prophecy. He is determined to stamp it out. He has good grounds for his vehement opposition as prophecy is so valuable to the church. God speaks through it. He brings edification, encouragement and consolation by means of it. Prophecy manifests the presence of God and brings conviction to the unsaved.

Through prophecy, God directs the actions of his people; he warns his people to escape from trouble; he prepares them to meet trouble; he points to those whom he wants in his service at home and overseas. Through prophecy, Christians can know the immediate will of God and copy Jesus' resolution to do only what he heard and saw the Father doing. Even if it takes another twenty-five years, we need to establish a vital and recognized role for prophets and prophecy. I believe that both the leaders and the people must do several things to establish this place.

The leaders

Those who prophesy must be confident that the leaders will treat their prophesying seriously, and not regard it with patronizing smiles as a mild, harmless eccentricity:

'I had better let him say his little piece.'

Leaders must make a public response to the prophesying. They should not admit prophecy without admitting a means of dealing with it. At the moment most prophesying is met with an embarrassed silence, then quickly forgotten. I have suggested my understanding of a biblical way of dealing with prophecy. The 'two or three' prophecies and separation by 'others' removes the possibility of wrong pressure by a strong-minded individual.

The leaders must stop ignoring prophecy. This is Paul's comment in 1 Thessalonians 5:20. In their services they should establish a biblical 'decently and orderly' exercising of gifts, ensuring that these principles are known and abided by, and then allow room for experimentation and failure. We learn by making mistakes, not by doing nothing. The pathway to maturity lies through the jungle of adolescent immaturity. This needs constant articulation.

It is a fundamental error to restrict the gifts to some lesser gathering like housegroups or after-meetings. Room must be made at all gatherings. This takes time. Mistakes must be acknowledged with a smile. It is most helpful to provide some sort of commentary or explanation for what has happened, and to make sugestions about what should happen next. Leaders should ensure a *taxis*—order and orderliness—to the services, and not permit a free for all, with spontaneity worshipped as a false god.

The leaders must know Scripture and be ready and able to defend sound doctrine, or expose false doctrine. They should assess the character of the person prophesying to prevent infiltration by false prophets, for the tests are for false prophets, not false prophesy. But Balaam's ass must constantly be borne in mind. If God can speak through a donkey, he can surely speak through funny old Mrs Ramsbottom and a pimply teenager. Beginners need constant encouragement to go on trying. They need guidance on how to stop as well.

Finally, leaders must set the example in public *zelotes* for prophecy. If the leaders clearly desire prophecy, it will come. If they are thought to be against it, God will pour out the blessing elsewhere.

The people

We must saturate ourselves in God's word. Prophetic inspiration is by our exposure to the word or our openness to the Spirit, and only very rarely by spontaneous verbal transmission. We need to pore over the Bible to hear most of what God wants us to speak out. As we do this, we must consciously align ourselves with the teaching of the Bible. I find it a horrible temptation to opt for understanding rather than obedience. We must be zealous for the gift of prophecy to be established in our church. Without any ambition for ourselves, we must offer ourselves to God to act in obedience to the prompting of his Spirit. All God needs is a mouth. We should offer to be his spokesperson,

Harold Pumfrey – a member of St Wilfrid's, Lower Willingdon, E. Sussex

Harold, a timid, retired ambulance driver, was filled with the Spirit when he attended a conference at Ashburnham Place in October 1977. This was too high-powered for him and by mid-week he had spiritual indigestion. So he tendered his apology for missing the evening session and went to his room to sleep.

As Harold settled down he began to hear 'words' in his mind and felt an urgent desire to write. He was not sure what to do and had no idea what was happening. He took up his pen and then felt compelled to write these words.

> I am the Lord God, and your Heavenly Father, and I love you, and I long for you to overcome your prejudices and your preconceived ideas. I do love you and I long to fill you with my love, so that you may be full to overflowing. And there will be such a change in your life that your face will shine with the light of my love, and all men will say, 'Surely he is with the Lord,' and will praise your Father in heaven.

Harold says, 'I was mystified. I did not understand what had occurred. Nothing like it had ever happened before. Yet I was sure it was not for me personally. So I asked two friends for advice. They believed it was a prophecy and should be shown to the conference leader. He agreed, and asked me to read it to the conference. It was a moving experience and I recall being anxious as to why God had bothered with someone like me. I feared it was all a mistake.'

Since that first prophetic message, Harold has allowed the Lord to develop the gift within him, and he has been used in similar, and more specific ways with considerable regularity.

to the world or to the church. There must be thorough preparation by prayer and fasting. Nothing can be accomplished without these twin disciplines.

Once we become serious about prophecy, we must expect God to speak to us, to summon us into his presence, to whisper his thoughts in our ears. It is most helpful to have a notebook and to cultivate the habit of recording those dreams, thoughts, words which we think might be God's word for us to repeat. If the Lord seems to suggest something which does not appear to be for us personally, then we should assume it is a prophecy to be passed on to another—either privately or in a service. These gifts should not be surrounded by such an aura that we think they rarely happen. God wants lots of prophesying. He desires the whole church to prophesy and that includes us! When the suspicion of a prophecy starts to grow, we must allow ourselves to be directed by him as to the place, time and person. We must trust ourselves implicitly to the Lord who will prompt us as to the where, when, who and what. It is important not to act on our own, but to function in pairs. Our thoughts should be shared with at least one other for their guidance, comment and support.

Most of us get very frightened at the point of delivery. It is good to identify the cause of the fear in order to ask God to deal with it. Am I afraid of what others will think, or of being unable to finish the prophecy, or even of saying something silly? Am I afraid of people, or of appearing foolish? We must be more afraid of what God thinks if we fail to speak out, than of what others will say if we do. We must absorb into our thinking the fact that we will only develop by failing, not by remaining silent. We must sympathize with each other and put up with each other's stumblings and inadequate attempts. We learn by practice, not by reticence. So let us get on with prophesying. Let us remove the gag from our mouths; offer ourselves as willing messengers; plead for the purification, inspiration and equipping of the Spirit; intercede for a partner in this holy task; and so allow the voice of God to be heard with clarity, authority and power.

In writing this book I have been struck by the complete absence—it seems to me—of any man currently holding the office of prophet in Great Britain. This should not be so. Our sad and declining nation needs a true prophet to sound forth God's word. I could suggest a few who aspire to that office, but their ambition should be to prophesy, not to become a prophet. It should be a matter for the most urgent intercession that God should both call and raise up some men especially and specifically for this task; and also that he thwart any ambitious interlopers. We need a British Bonhoeffer, a Luther King, or a Tutu. We need another Wilberforce, Shaftesbury or Booth in this our generation.

I have also been saddened by the great confusion about the ministry of prophet. The growing clericalism within Restoration circles has led to the common idea that anyone with a prophetic ministry must be male, a full-time preacher, and a member of an apostolic team. They have so confused the office and the ministry that they are in danger of ending up with neither, just long-winded preachers. The clearest example of a prophet in East Sussex is a quantity surveyor who rarely preaches and has only recently been given any office in his church. The prophet I most trust is a housewife who has never preached and who has no position in her church whatsoever.

Every Spirit-filled Christian can prophesy, and the man or woman with a ministry is simply the one who prophesies most frequently. We need a prophetic church and we need men and women with the ministry of prophet in every local church; God will use anybody who is willing to seek his face, seek his gifts and be bold enough to give it a try.

I said: 'What a wretched state I am in! I am lost, for I am a man of unclean lips and I live among a people of unclean lips, and my eyes have looked at the King, Yahweh Sabaoth.'

Then one of the seraphs flew to me, holding in his hand a live coal which he had taken from the altar with a pair of tongs. With this he touched my mouth and said: 'See now, this has touched your lips, your sin is taken away, your iniquity is purged.'

Then I heard the voice of the Lord saying: 'Whom shall I send? Who will be our messenger?'

I answered, 'Here I am, send me.'

He said: 'Go.'

Isaiah 6:5–9